ALSO BY JEFF CLARK *The Little Door Slides Back*

Music and Suicide

Music and Suicide

Jeff Clark

Farrar Straus Giroux

New York

Farrar, Straus and Giroux
19 Union Square West, New York 10003

Distributed in Canada by Douglas & McIntyre Ltd.
Printed in the United States of America
Published in 2004 by Farrar, Straus and Giroux
First paperback edition, 2005

Some of these works originally appeared in *Angle*,
Chicago Review, *Explosive*, *Faucheuse*, *The Hat*,
Mirage #4/Periodical, *nearSouth*, *Poetry Review*
(London), *Purple*, and *Yen Agat*, and in the following
volumes: *Sun on 6*, illustrated by Jasper Johns (Z Press,
2000); and *Arab Rab* (Seeing Eye Books, 1999).

The Library of Congress has cataloged
the hardcover edition as follows:
Clark, Jeff, 1971–
    Music and Suicide / Jeff Clark. — 1st ed.
        p. cm.
    ISBN 0-374-28145-9 (alk. paper)
        I. Title.

    PS3603.L3645M87 2004
    813.'6—dc22

                        2003060847

Paperback ISBN-13: 978-0-374-52959-8
Paperback ISBN-10: 0-374-52959-0

www.fsgbooks.com

10 9 8 7 6 5 4 3 2 1

For Susan Clark

Geoffrey G. O'Brien

and

Stephen Walrod

Contents

Music and Suicide

A Chocolate and a Mantis

The phosphorous cheeks of an ailing jester fallen that day
from an alien haze over jade lanes
to blades arrayed in ribboned mazes
created to flay a dilated spirit hole
He was a chaotic boy with phosphorous cheeks
and a glistening sphinctral sanctity
a violet fallen alloy of a Medium
and a gigolo to sleep
He was white waste of nebula-scented hours
fallen that day an alien length
to a place of stale rain and that day
to crawl crying to the side
was to harvest no more eggs of fantasy strewn out horizontally
and found by following a hare that could be a guide or a lie in fur
He was ugly when he ate the eggs, and in a trance
a chocolate and a mantis sat on his thigh
and said that Even broken or swollen
hysterical inside long boxes or on wires
or swallowing gray fay lures

to take and decompose both your lapel rose and the hose that fed it
you must offer a mantis your hand, a chocolate your tongue
then never again ill use or even dream to curate
fake faces or oases or their words

And sometimes you rejoice because you dream
and are engaged with a wet bottom
but dreamless to find that your senses are weaker
and you could feel no cigarette or Ra
no tilting park or clef
but the chaos of a sac of cracked slides
and scales, sucked-to-death larks and stabbing swings
and you knew that if you could be a jester bred to beg dream for eggs
if you could see a Jesus singing from a tree his own father grew
you could polish all of a cellar with spit
or hold the shined tile of your face to a suffocated street this Sunday
or sometimes to the crown of two real or even two envisioned thighs
blessed by suburban or country perfumes

because sometimes you contorted to kiss the side of a false staff
and you dreamt you were decomposing
were dooming your face
to have wanted to kiss a stick in a mirage

and not a marigold harem or a brown crown
You saw madness was to love a woman you extracted from a tale
of man-made everglades in which masqueraders play
and get sprayed from the cars of a passing parade
because sometimes your face tasted of the taint of those papers
    of escape
and psychic counts dictated your fainting or what you would trust

Sometimes you reclined so mistily on the wet lips of states
so shimmeringly on states
that a specter slid up a gold or silver surface
you never leveled until it possessed and emptied you
and now escapes to exist in other ethers

because what is to be burned
is equally unpresent in your urns and blurs

A Corpse More Constant Than Hearts

I still looked for you   strangled
that single spring day of all lies   by the side of a skyscraper
From behind came a seagull throwing up berries
we leaned where a shadow began to climb
Do you know why I wanted to kill you?   I wanted to sleep
There are strong veins and money for any moment you would visit
The vice of vines, gun in red sun
Now a hearse at the curb
Is there freshness in the driver's questions
Was there pain in strangling   was there a clock
    was there more pain the warm morning
                          that followed strangling
at the top of which a three-quarter moon receded
to the south and further down a jet, still further down were clouds
Did strangling have a sound, did you think at all of painting

Like Cats Coming out of Clocks

Channeled for a periled girl
at the intersection of 2nd & C in a memory
Like cats coming out of clocks
Three seconds so a voice says
Like cats coming out of clocks
to fly so my eyes never find you again
from the Golden Gate to a range of saline
Like cats coming out of clocks
Or mistaken seers now gone foresaw a drop in a closet
Like cats coming out of clocks
But a parallel barrel obliterates a pearl
A parallel barrel resonates a pool in a garden
that dries and leaves alkali
Like cats coming out of clocks
You saw a lily tilt when you were ill
Like cats coming out of clocks
Or a hummingbird struck from the air in Oroville

You were defending petals from the hovering hoses
that surrounded the loud canal
    Like cats coming out of clocks
Objects in the hallways here will rot
but where you go will you prey on the jubilant voices
    Like cats coming out of clocks
of the Prancing Princes who lock us in trances of panic
    Like cats coming out of clocks
First kill the Prince who sells this memory of an hour
back to the memory's owner
whose friend's hours were sold
to a rust orphanage in a fragrant orange grove
untended since the first breath
of the barrel or the mouth of the girl
who strewed the seeds
or strung the string through wet beads

Cama

for Lizi

So much is unknown, yesterday my life began
and tonight wants to remain here
again no choice but to begin
by writing what is continuously seen
pink silk pillow with black and gold diamonds
rings at the edges
Your profile in a picture, momentary heat
bruise at the outside top of a thigh
Bread and chocolate, blue nails
and in these words is nothing
that will satisfy me
Russet light in which I first touched you
pool-blue sheets, bedpillows cased in a goldenrod color
a belt and scarf draped over the headboard

Wellings and smells embellish the bed
Do you hear the music in that line?
Why not remove it? Why remove it?
Art is permissible sickness

Laughter and slight torment, liquids, cherry-red robe
Where are you tonight?
Where should I go? New music plays
the same black ink as last year
same cheap pen with which other words
I want this bed to be almost empty, no longer want
to be part of my lines, no desire
to be anywhere
only to kiss your eyes again
pupils and irises singular
Seers and haunters

Now we're beginning to hurt
I continuously lose you
I want to ask you something
will ask you tomorrow
Outside this bed, something else prevails
cleverly veils

Your face so unlike what I desired in winter
Comprehensions are hectic, Eastern descriptions
of senses without contortion

meaning for me now only more glass
coarse black hair and gazelle-like legs

Longing to leave but learning to meditate
Seams and delusional motes
Enlightened, slowly, or being driven madder
Both at once, the text says

further into disharmony, by this bed, by your legs
lips mixed with sickish music
No correspondence between
this writing and your face

Dilator

What I was lacking you brought back
                    I was building a clean, strong structure
and it cracked

        I was untangling a lady's medicated braids
as she sought surplus purple for a gamay garment

Your money always shared in prescription store aisles
                while malevolent mimes

                        aimed hoses into the ocean
with things burning right beside

But your eyes and words were sucked yesterday through blinds
over waves and daydream-made azure ghats

                We scaled spires and gutted ourselves
Blue light spied through a gloryhole

Tan transmitter dismantled
and waning white noise escapes the collapsed baths

Green grams fanned through air
and the irrigation corps

                              dessicates in stations
A vaulted sky violent with nimbus symptoms
an ambulance tremulates lengthening silences

We never quieted cries or shot at odious offshore ships
                        Sick fractured voices from vaporous places
No longer even questions but the sound of questioning

Memories of azalea-colored lips that suck well
A woman who painted dosage boats,
trauma-dowsing dunes, flora flares

Her tongue a hoe of astral agriculture
The diceholes fill with dew,
    her designs with lobal foam and beams

In an orchid store
Deranging rays, the fluttering inverted comb,
   softly bouncing snout
              of a dead sea horse
in a tank with darting disks and oval pieces

Blood does not accrue but moves
       You pretend there is
   something in the sand the water wants
backwash ramming incoming blue walls
past the bridge a black ship on glassy resins

Cunning things thrive in sunless dungeons
      No longer her songs but the ache of playing

Pearls augment the neck of a woman in this park
an Asian boy chases a rolling melon

Our antitheses drain cathedrals with droll catheters
   meant to clean

Missing Is a Stimulant

a circuit, bled memory
a séance of the veins, a liquid hinge
Deceit, the tones of dreamed sceneries
defaced by a single face
the day itself more marred
by these traces of fragrance
chances to fathom her absence
or collapse with the sap of plants
and sleep, and demand of a jasmine-scented face
How are you still so fragrant?
An object at a morgue or an organ

First Pastoral

Imagine if you can a miniature pageant on a hill
and picture then with me a boy
who's on a stool, a punished fool
and a panelist pours out his pleas
Removes his orange shirt
removes his face's glaze and bedtime insights
Lays him on the runway and laughs
Just yesterday this panelist had killed a dog
    and cum in a lily cup

and the others say, Bend for us, spin around
Cry, sneeze, drown
and the lily cup in the boy's dream
    is fed again

Imagine if you will a pageant on a hill
and picture if you can a boy
designed to be impaled upon a stilt
and bleed for a panelist's joy

G Major Quay

Now I write it in verse for the last time: birds found on the ground
form a grid of lost times
and the grass beside untended corpses still climbs
the best set and forum, looking down

I have been to the opera twice, a cloud in a warm climate
sitting where all work remains to be done
June sun so forthcoming that to see him in the sand oval alone
denies songs as being the perfect fit

that arcane tone flatlines in the aftermath of the poem
the helmet of daylight taken off
as white cotton of blossom motif from a tuft
and to know this one is to know them

again in the loge a fifth visit. Opera neither soft nor unsafe
seldom about work or the haste of lines
but belladonna and the bullman about to disorganize
for the last time . . . the audience repairs to a sunny café

called the Deaf Man's Hands, down Quay Elém and to the right
specializing in dove and waves off the sea
drinks are served and a painter tries to say
This is the first picture of the last night

WITH GEOFFREY G. O'BRIEN

Shiva Hive

When I look at you, I see someone who loves another so deeply, so purely and marvelously, that I must always thank Chance I am permitted to know, through you, that love.

Can you tell me: is it a capacity that existed within you before you ever existed ... or is it, instead, the fortune of your having encountered one whom you could so love, one who could be so loved?

Your question makes me uncomfortable. You are idealizing, and therefore distorting, something or someone. You are engaging in a flight of fancy that, whether you realize it or not, is the shape that love itself takes. To love and to imagine are one and the same thing. An opening to what can never be fully present. If I were to confess any capacity to you, it would be the capacity to contain that opening, that emptiness. For loving has no meaning but "to be found wanting." Desire, also, is the rapturous study of distance. And the maintenance of this distance is an art that must be cultivated.

So is it your perpetual maintenance of this "distance" from that which you desire that is to be thanked for, at least, this marvelous love I see very clearly you have for someone; is it not, instead, sim-

ply that this someone has called this love in you into existence, and now, moment by moment, calls it out?

I leave my window open but the hummingbird—though it may hover near now and then—will never enter my room. You have the power "to contain that opening," while I, for my part, will cry that the hummingbird never comes in, or someday I'll trap and either cage it, or kill it. How then to get to where you are—or learn to contain "the not," the "opening"?

You are still idealizing. You attribute to me the possession of a secret, a position of mastery that I have to reject. You "see very clearly" what you want to see; it is a "marvelous" picture. Yet, even if your picture fails to correspond to my reality, we can meet in the space of that failure. A space where none of the lines connect. Words like "pure" and "perpetual" are not appropriate here. We are not looking for a crystalline being, but for something in the process of melting. Allowing each of us to move within the otherness of the other. That is the condition of the possibility of Eros. (No object can give birth to love. Instead, love is the condition for the appearance of the object. An apparition that must be awaited in the way that a poet awaits the inspiration for a poem.)

I believe sometimes I see in your eyes the trace of—what?—a sorrow, perhaps even a profound sorrow. If I've not mis-seen, or

haven't merely intuited a false source of this trace, then may I ask:
does this sorrow derive from certain disappearances?

I recall that you wear no fragrance.

Nor do I usually rouge my cheeks. But when did you look into my eyes, searching for signs and symptoms? Of course, by asking me, you know you will receive only the authorized version of the story. Yet it seems you believe that, if you put your finger on my most vulnerable place — whether it be love or sorrow — I will be forced to admit the inadmissible. My dear, I would gladly admit everything to you, as far as I myself know it. But I'm afraid you would find my life story exceedingly banal. I admit to having a melancholic temperament; I could even attempt to explain my nature to you by citing causes both accidental and necessary. But I couldn't bear your disappointment on discovering my sameness. If you want to discover my otherness, you will have to invent it for yourself. It is precisely what I cannot tell you. (I only hope the story you invent for me won't rely on so simplistic a narrative as the Fall of Innocence, where a state of original happiness is undone by separation. Rather, I think melancholia is induced by making too many connections between things.)

I'm not thinking about melancholia — I'm thinking about the
envoy-children Death sends, who laugh disgustingly and bear little
blank scraps of paper. And I'm thinking about how you can help me

*learn how to send them back bruised, or shivering. But if you can-
not, for lack of words or lack of desire, will you tell me about love,
or phenomena equal to love?*

*This is the fortune I was given tonight at dinner at Chef Jia's:
"Hope for the best, but prepare for the worst."*

I may lack the words, but certainly not the desire to reply. I have the feeling that you want the finality of an absolute Answer. Perhaps, in a state of mystical ecstasy, such an Answer might be revealed, but such a state necessarily exceeds the limitations of language. And wanting to permanently inhabit the timeless silence of an absolute Answer is tantamount to a death wish, is it not? Here where we live, in the realm of matter in motion, everything is constantly coming into being and passing away and never exactly repeating itself. That is, reality is constantly improvising new shapes for itself, shapes that will never be finished or "perfected" before they vanish. Like death, the perfect circle is an abstraction that can only exist as an idea, not as a reality. Dying, of course, is all too real; it involves the transformation of a highly organized system into a much less organized residuum of atoms. But the flow of matter/energy also has shown itself to be capable of some miraculous transformations (see how the sun-swirl, after nearly five billion years, has transformed some of its substance into a mind-swirl, a language-swirl). I would recommend studying reality's own modes of improvisation and then working your own changes upon them, guided only by the open-endedness —by this, I mean the *unattainable otherness*— of your desires.

Will you tell me again that fairy tale about the child who follows a dragonfly out of her yard?

If you wish—but remember that nothing ever repeats itself exactly. This time the flight of the dragonfly was influenced by the gravitational field of distant galaxies. Seated at a table in the garden, the child heard the buzz of wings. The dragonfly's shadow slipped across the blank pages of the child's diary like a kind of ephemeral writing. Perhaps it wanted to write her life story. This time the child did not leave her yard in the usual way. She stared at the pages that had suddenly become blank again. It was the moment before creation.

Can you describe your conception of magnetics?

Magnetism is a kind of unliving memory of the time when everything was concentrated in a single, infinitely dense point. A time when you and I commingled, along with the rest of the future. Now certain things long to be reunited with one another by way of magnetism, while others choose the path of electricity. Every visible object thus tends to be haunted by an invisible field, just as we ourselves are suspended by voices.

> *Magnetics = nostalgia for union. Electrics = yearning for states of unreciprocative transmitting ...? Could it be said your being an electrician has to do with the transits of your first two decades?*

When will you cease hectoring me with your questions? I know only that not even nothing is identical to itself. There is no peace to be found, not even in non-existence, which fails to negate its own negativity. It cannot forbid itself the leap into existence. Of course, the actual sequence of events would be different in every universe. In our local continuum, for example, the present seems to have finally overtaken the future. In contrast to this, my "first two decades" coincided with a time when revolution was in the air.

  . . .

If no further questions are forthcoming from you, I'll ask myself the Last Question. "Why is there something rather than nothing?" I believe I answered that already: if nothing had the power to negate even itself, it would become something. The fact that we are experiencing something is proof that the power of nothing is complete —that it consummates (and hence, consumes) itself as something. This is perhaps only a syntactic trick, yet the form of the question

("Why?") presumes that any solution will be carried out at the level of language. At the level of experience, the world is in conflagration.

Now that I am alone, I find myself becoming more voluble. May I close with a prayer? It is, of course, the prayer of an unbeliever, and so must be called a "Fantastic Prayer" (I borrow this title from a German Dadaist). The following text is the first in a series of such *Phantastische Gebete*.

> Signs of the flock returning.
> —flicker
> at the standstill of certainty.

> Cavern where the words were stained.

> Entrance
> the imperative
> to pour this trace.

> Chalice, couch.
> Anthill, whore.

> Dust, desire
> is the rapturous study of distance.

What do you think of the twins Obsession and Devotion?

I'm back from a vacation on Neptune, so to speak, otherwise I would have replied sooner. (Neptune is a blue orb at the very edge of the solar system, moving amongst families of ice. And it glows inside itself, as explained by equations that are akin to music.)

Your question, in Neptunian terms, wants to rotate around a center, the point of unity of "Obsession" and "Devotion." It asserts a family relation. But I doubt the two conditions ever shared the same womb. They are mutually annihilative, as hole & whole. Obsession is made of emptiness, and Devotion of fulfillment. Obsession is ruled by compulsion, whereas Devotion is an act of free will. Obsession stuffs itself and still can't get enough, while Devotion offers its gift as a continual & inexhaustible outpouring. Obsession is an impoverished state, Devotion an impossibly rich one. Obsession desperately needs to consume & appropriate the life-force of its object; Devotion takes nothing but brings everything.

However, this table of antinomies is all too neat. Neither "Obsession" nor "Devotion" is an eternal essence; rather, they are particular ways of constructing human experience, arising from the chaos pattern of history. "Obsession," a relatively new construction, can only arise in exploded, alienated societies suffering from a scarcity of love & solidarity; whereas "Devotion" is a much older form of consciousness, echoing with deep harmonic overtones, & based on rituals of mutual recognition & respect. Yet even though it's older, Devotion is pregnant with the future, & points beyond the human; while Obsession is doomed to repeat the present.

Of course, Obsession often walks around transparently disguised as Devotion. Whereas true Devotion has no need to exhibit itself as such.

If, for some unfortunate reason, a subject cannot eliminate, or alter, its obsessional mechanism, and must therefore continue to lead an existence of emptiness, compulsion, all those things you so aptly mention — is it right for this subject to place any hope in the possibility that certain of its objects will learn to find ample nourishment from its other qualities?

Or do you think (as I now cannot, myself, help but wonder) that most of the subject's other dominant qualities are too interwoven with Obsession to be free enough for an object to isolate and derive sustenance from?

You have the right to demand recognition by the other. But you have no right to seek completion by means of the other. You will always be incomplete. (This statement is not a condemnation, but another way of saying that the world cannot contain itself.)

You once told me you would write down for me the story of the man who looked into a mirror and didn't see himself.

Once again, forgive my delay in replying—I've been burdened with the indexing of Newton's *Principia*. (The laws of falling bodies seem to describe a tragedy—though not everything that falls experiences impact. Think of orbiting, tracing out a trance.) I'm hardly in a position to write the story you requested.

Still, if we remember the mirror is a resistant medium, our faces, along with our thoughts, will travel much more slowly toward their images. "Recognition," a dark drapery sinking through the mirror's water, will settle gradually upon our eyes. The mask of recognition is donned for the (always awkward, always premature) encounter with our mirror-self.

It's the same with words: to delay the arrival of a word's meaning, say it over and over and over again until its true identity appears, wrested free of language. The same experiment can be conducted with the gaze, trained steadily upon one's mirror-image. After a while, only the eyes remain alive behind the mask. If the spell is prolonged, only a laminated pattern or pool of light pulses through the eternal instant.

No doubt these are obvious and primitive means of misrecognition—I only mention them to point out how easily the membrane is transpierced that separates us from the unnameable. But the unnameable is also the uninhabitable—and so, huddled here in our temporary homes, we keep its hiding-places (a book, a mirror) for future reference.

Now, O my Interrogator, I have a question for you: What, in non-Newtonian terms, is the "solid of least resistance"?

The solid of least resistance is a bullet.

But my fantasy is more often drawn to water. There was—and is, but differently—a bridge that connected my old home with another county.

A bullet would shatter a mirror. And, with velocity, a mirror would shatter itself on the water beneath the bridge. Yet it is water one uses to clean a mirror, while a bullet would never be used to clean a mirror.

Just before I arranged myself and papers here in bed, it was a kind of water, its release, that permitted me to no longer fantasize a solid of least resistance, or anything about my old home.

In my opinion, a mirror is stronger than a bullet. Can a bullet fire at itself? A mirror can and does. The mirror poses the problem of self-relation, a problem that remains even after its physical embodiment has been shattered, or dropped into the river.

The problem of self-relation involves a higher level of awareness, an awareness of awareness. Try firing a bullet at the word "of." The bullet may obliterate the mark, but the word itself is not removed from language. In any case, the problem of self-relation resembles a (bullet) hole as much as it does a mirror. You can't know that you exist unless you're self-divided.

That is, unless you're self-mirrored or language-riddled. But is it possible to be bullet-mirrored?

You seem to want to privilege release over reflection. I want to say—since in this case I am your mirror—that reflection is a higher form of release, a way of being bullet-mirrored.

Bullet-mirrored. A Shiva Hive. Destroying building. Let me recite for you a couplet from Shelley's "Epipsychidion":

But soft and fragrant is the faded blossom,
And it has no thorn left to wound thy bosom.

And let me translate this couplet into this evening's language:

But cold and flagrant the unoiled revolver,
And there is no bullet left to fill its chamber.

A bosom is a blossom with excised "l" and "s." "Alas." Late last night I spoke with a woman who had invited me to accompany her to a northern beach this weekend. I told her I wouldn't, after all, be able to join her. But what I didn't tell her — and she is the one I've fantasized accompanying for months now — is that I would be staying in this weekend because of incommunicable torment. Her reply:

"Alas."

"Bullet-mirrored" — as if something lethal and invisible were speeding deafeningly, infinitely, toward one's bosom, and though never penetrating it, perpetually screaming, alarming, threatening. And if only one could learn to give total attention to this terrifying noise, this stationary shrieking blur, one might hope to someday diffuse it.

Since I left my home I have remembered only one nightmare. Its setting is bright blue early morning. I cross from the bedroom door of my old home, through the living room, toward the bathroom. The bathroom door is open and before me is the medicine cabinet mirror. In it I see the upper body and beautiful, white-blue face of M. She has hung herself from the wall just beside the bathroom doorway. We're both, therefore, facing the mirror. My sensations upon fathoming her image there are an admixture of intense longing, ineffable pleasure that she has elected to suicide in my own home, and premature embarrassment that I won't be able to weep before my mother, who is now emerging from my bedroom doorway in her nightgown, her face beginning to contort.

I notice this blue tableau of two women (or one woman, mirror-divided, and discovered at a time of mourning?) is inversely symmetrical to the couplet about the impotent gun. Remember, I too am your mirror, your M.

The blossom is a shrieking blur in my bosom. It is the sound of Allah's moon-cry, "all less" before "alas."

The figures in your nightmare are sad because they are recognizable.

To the extent they are not recognizable, they are beautiful.

An object rejected by all categories is, by definition, unrecognizable: "There was once a man whose mirror failed him . . ."

A warning: do not place your hopes in the idea of "total attention," which, as a mirror-relation, can never see the back of its own head.

To realize itself, even "torment" must contain what it is not.

Alas, the world is constantly revising and erasing its propositions. At the mercy of these tides, we long for the unauthored . . .

Jade Ache

I address myself only to those persons capable of hearing me.
MARQUIS DE SADE

Anyway, whatever . . . It's effortless.
Ticker is long, like a subway ride
to a distant lampshade dealer.
Smoke, and if
they decide to open it, it writes, and they read.
A dollar a day adds up—
and why shouldn't it? It, too, has
little else in mind, the subway
shakes the house a bit, the cat
has a kind of dreamy Chinese anxiety by
an irate hibiscus, though we don't know this for sure
since the hibiscus and the cat are merely in a kind of painting,
it's hard to tell . . .
Elegance, ambivalence, wit,
manipulativeness, erudition.
Lunch ends and they think that if they
were in the west they'd fill the days with sailing,
or an oxblood red where now one finds floral paper and
    fine veneer,

maybe a different school where there'd be
a different telephone number.
It's that I know this young man again whose sentences
evoke jade ache and the impromptu of MC Endless
yet whose desire is unlike mine,
cease to be and be at peace.
Nevertheless it happens that we squeeze
dancers between us and make "sandwiches."
Six, eight times, a German girl, a brunette from way back
but never her friend in magenta polka dots. I am remembering
this and the subway shakes the third floor again.
The melancholy bedside arrangement at 2:18 a.m.

I have to go on—
but where to? Up there, down here,
something you would agree with? Whatever.
Flocks will forage forever in toy-blue orchards.
He felt it happen, sort of. This morning.
Or was it yesterday morning.
One of them awakened and saw for the first time
it could be anything, anything at all,
and that was the beauty of it.
And it was only beautiful.

A payphone rang.

"Hello?" they answered.

"Will you listen to me for five or so minutes?" the voice at the other end asked.

"No," they said, and didn't hang up.

Sun on 6

Nurse of terminal birds   of blistered lily   No black sun aristocrat
fantasy   Red rays beat on wet bed and dead palm   Caustic powder
Fear pulse   Siphon blood to themes in perishing shadow   A relic
propped against sunflame   Wall wet   Red light   Mustard-colored
stinking stocking   Warm fur   Fear pulse   Sun on 6   Cheek sweat
on picture glass   Sunbaked butterfly crushed   Catholic figure with
broken head   Vulgar picture curling   Fear pulse   Metal lock chest
Sun on 6   Sick friend   Sunburned boy over bird carcass   Black other
room   Open legs   Shasta murmur   Serpent shape   Throbbing
tongue   Sunbleached ribbon   Wet seat   Brown blade   Fear pulse
Oaxacan pillbox   Sun on 6   All my probable sighs broiling in a stiff
throat it dries to have life   Fear pulse   Hearing is a faucet   The brutal
is lasting   Mouth foam   White spots   View spun   Fear pulse
Thought nausea   Sun on 6   Seizure in receding shade   It taunts
my throat   Quince battered by orange magnets   My groin steams
I search for a child's party   Dead scent pass I'm moving   Iris
embalmed   Brutal beam hunts shadow terminals   Butterfly fled
the rays   False trance of squares   Circle burns

Teheran

Raccoons digging frantically at something, nighttime, stretch of lawn in the desert, down a ways to the left on grass another raccoon is dead or sleeps. Almost step on it.

Construction site, truck ascends nearly vertical ramp.

Girls fighting in an indoor pool.

Tick bite on the hip, behind my belt, in a beige field. Kill it by tapping it gently with a stick.

Bong, Hispanic boy, magic trick.

Father and infant daughter drowning in black viscous churning pool. Trying to save the man, knowing the girl has drowned. Holding X's hand, lower myself into the whirlpool, feel the man's stiff shoulder.

Walking in and out of shops trying to find a pen with which to write down the words "Beauty Hunter."

She has snuck out again. In the morning, her coat discovered hanging on top of my coat. She awakens, gives me head, bites my cock lightly just below the head.

In the ocean, big waves, with a childhood friend, as well as two young boys, as if Siamese twins. They appear and disappear, pursue me, are right beside me then yards away, sinister giggling, I swim into an immense wave, feigning fearlessness, am propelled over the top of them. All the while am trying to hold aloft, out of the water, an oil paintbrush. Now there are seals encircling me, which I understand means there are also sharks, but feign fearlessness still. The water is warm.

Walking out to the furthest possible border of a moor or bog, mudplain, swamp, trying not to get my sneakers dirty. Someone tries to tell me, hands cupped around mouth, a ways away, to go no further. I keep on, and finally, step by step, sink waist-deep. Terrified. It's very dark out, but as if lit by artificial bluish light.

Look into a mirror. The front gums of my bottom jaw are hideously blackened, blood-caked, pussing. Looks like dark, wet soil, with flecks of meat, pimples.

Sucking sound from a dry drain.

Airplane falling out of the sky. Giving X head, her sex is strange, the labia unfold illogically.

A cat on its back, having been tossed, or having fallen, down the side of a gravel slope beside a surface road. I study it, thinking it has rigor mortis. It begins to quiver. Gets up, scampers off. Gray and white, long hair.

In bed, holding in my joined palms a pink, waving, spiny, anemone-like creature. Frightened by it, but entranced. It leaps from my hands onto the bedsheet, shimmies to the side of the bed, down into the crevice between bed and wall.

X proposes a ménage in a hyperbolic, supra-poetic letter.

I marry a senior citizen, realize slowly, disgust mounting, it is a mistake to have done so.

A man and I, in a Burmese restaurant, see a fat black spider floating at the surface of a small aquarium. He puts his face to the water to let the spider attach to it. Pulls his face out of the water, dripping. On his cheek is a ladybug, which is still for a moment before flying off.

Ride a motorcycle into a house, up a staircase, into a little room where two couples are cooing at babies in prams. I excuse myself overpolitely and maneuver the motorcycle through the room, down the stairs and back outside.

Mom and Dad screwing, she looking back at me.

Meet someone named Jeff Clark.

Trying to escape, by moving terribly slowly, backwards, a man trying to load, aim his gun, shoot me. Finally fires, keeps missing. Am struggling toward a car, jump in it.

In a helicopter flying low over an everglade or swamp filled with scores of crocodiles.

Trying to hide from a precocious baby.

In a backyard, beating (tapping) two lizard-like creatures on the head with a stick, as if to kill them decently, politely. Each has a small egg in its jaws. They finally die and, ashamed, begin to dig, with a large shovel, a grave in which to bury them. Stop once the hole seems big enough to contain them, then understand I must dig yet deeper. Unearth a football. If it's an antique, I'll give it to X. But it's not. Then unearth a coffee mug with a man's face on it.

Telephone message from X. "The apartment above me is for rent if you're interested, but the kitchen and bathroom and all the closets are padlocked, so really it's just a single bedroom," her voice cracking.

Street beginning to flood, torrents, rain pouring from the sky, waves forming and breaking hugely in the distance, an Afghan dead, smeared on road, the same one I'd seen roaming unleashed inside a supermarket.

Walking through a desert pocked with very small hills. Lay damp towels over miniature smoldering fires. Little clumps of unnaturally green, as if neon, grass that doesn't burn.

Clinging to the side of a mud cliff, in a storm, above a washed-out gulley, watch a leopard or jaguar teach her kittens to snatch carp-like fish from the rainpools. Looks up, spies me hanging above her, returns to fishing without alarm.

Swim out into huge, dark gray storm surf, great whites, rogue sets. Look back and X is attempting to follow me out. Sky suddenly darkens. Shout, No, you'll die too.

Helping a little girl scale an absurdly tall chain-link fence.

Swimming in beautiful blue ocean, bright sun, a lifeguard shouts through a megaphone that everyone must exit the water at once. I swim quickly to the beach, climb to the top of the bluff overlooking the sea. Men come out of black vans with furious, gnashing dogs that strain at their leashes. The men, dressed in dark blue one-piece jumpsuits, are overheard saying that a whale-sized crocodile had been spotted approaching the beach in Area 14. The dogs descend the bluff and thrash into the water. See the submerged shadow of the crocodile turn away from the dogs and swim back out to sea. Remember it was Area 14 in which I'd been swimming.

Bird singing, clings to a wall inside a house. Flies about from room to room, I chase after it. Then it speaks to me, in English, darts to a far corner of the room into which I've followed it, becomes a kitten.

Looking out back door of apartment. Gorillas foraging in lush foliage. I throw dirt stones at them. They become agitated, then enraged. As soon as they've almost reached me, I slam door shut.

Jumping up and down in a field of dead grass, hollow sound beneath my feet, a man saying that probably there is a lion den beneath. Lions have been killing raccoons, who rid the field of rats, he therefore wants the lions shot. Follow him a ways into a concrete drainage tunnel beneath the field. He says, There are bones everywhere. I wade further into the tunnel behind him. Inside is an enormous, flooded basement, as if beneath an equally enormous apartment building. Cabinets, storage locker, bed frames, car parts, boxes, etc. He goes far in, wants me to follow, I don't.

Tumultuous waves and whitewater, don't want to but enter and begin to swim out, beneath the surface is coral and urchins and broken bottles, I can't dive beneath breaking waves, must submerge shallowly on my back, yet am hammered by a huge breaking wave, rolled over and over, skin shredded.

Paddling a long raft or surfboard through a dank lagoon, snake-like creatures beneath olive-green swampwater, am covered with thousands of mosquitos.

Hear X rummaging around inside closet situated on the opposite side of hallway wall I stare at. Aim a rifle at the sound of her, and fire. She stumbles from the room into the hallway, weeping. The bullet seems to have penetrated her heart. But she smiles, pulls the dress down off her shoulder, and in fact the bullet has only lightly grazed her bicep.

Partly camouflaged python in leafy loam in back yard. See a thick piece protrude from the dead leaves, coiling slowly. I kick at it with my boot then leap back. Then I spit, whistle at it, finally hit it with a rock. It stirs, then fully emerges, hissing, angered, is giant, absurdly so. Begins to slither away from me, has a thick bulge toward its tail. Has it just eaten a cat? At the edge of the yard it transforms into a tiger, turns back, leers at me, roars. I hurry, terrified, to the house. A young boy smirks from within a sliding-glass door, refuses to unlock it.

Read a nonexistent chapter of *A Lover's Discourse* which concerns those evenings when the lover has disappeared without leaving a note.

In a forest with X, looking for arrowheads. Keep finding tiny speckled eggs, broken, at the base of tall pine trees. Have all fallen, some cracked, some shattered, many with dead blue jay chicks protruding from the shells. Hear a faint buzzing from inside a tree, put my ear to it, listen closely.

In a random apartment, older man enters with grocery bags and says the best way to quit drugs is to have a nice white girlfriend. A young woman enters the apartment, followed by a young man, who pulls out his cock. Young woman walks over and kneels, about to give him head. X comes into the room then, excited, talking noisily, says to him, taking his cock from the young woman and stroking it, "You can only put it in up to the R."

Succumb

I lay on a blanket in the warm grass. The green of the garden, the trees, the grass, was honeyed by sun. You were lying beside me, facing the chest-high fava bean plants. I slowly pulled your white cotton dress across your bottom. A breeze from the bay pushed pollen from the boughs above us into the air. I smelled and nuzzled the skin now also breeze-struck and honeyed, imperceptibly attentive. Amberish spots. I swept my face from a very faintly fragrant, partly shadowed, and strawberry-textured alcove down behind a knee and kissed the line there. I heard your newspaper settle against the grass. The bottoms of your feet were light orange and grass-stained and smelled of wood and dirt and sunsweat. Your toenails were painted a plum shade.

Brief circular panic of breeze-struck five-pointed white blossoms I now know are called nicotiana. Tall singular stalks. I took my mouth from your toes, lay on my back beside you again, closed my eyes, and imagined myself seated on a dark gray pillow in this room of reddening consciousness and azure.

A window facing north and a window facing east. Through the north window I see ginger and walnuts, apartments, a pearly angled surface, a woman's back, hilltops, purple and yellow irises, a friend's mother, a beige wall with mothstain. Something outside the window that faces east confuses me, as it always has. I take a piece of paper from my shirt pocket, unfold it, and say the words scribbled on it: arise, coalesce, disappear. I think of love that is coming and of dropping into water. No one wants to succumb, and yet one would. To give out.

In the window that faces north, the only transparent window at this moment, I see an unadulterated web and the fig tree, bare throughout winter, that has guzzled sun and is now so full with leaves that I can no longer be seen by the shape that would move at night in its own window there across two yards.

A lemon tree reminds me of a woman whose letter arrived yesterday and who is tormented almost continually by the past. Like her I dream of autonomy from memory and prediction. She wants to know if memory that makes one ache is not memory at all but weakness that would like to linger forever in the company of certain images. Through the north window I see a picnic table on whose surface move shapes of light and shadow. Is it true that if she dies I would absorb any of her energy?

Alongside a fantasy of harmony I set one of sex and lie back.

The fig tree is a conductor, a screen, a tree, a medium, nothing yesterday, a crystal ball. I see a cobbled alley where I once looked for someone, I see my friend again. She is powerful, and I hear a fragment from a proverb: She can make a flower grow. She can make a flower die.

The fig tree is one of the sun's mirrors. I see a crescent of hair I slowly exposed to orange sunlight and kissed. In the fig tree a puppet is tangled. I see a woman fearful of rooms without sufficient light.

There is another window. A small one that pushes open like a door. Fava beans were eaten, fennel root, peppers, wild rice, meat. Much calm and affectionate talk, satiation, warm air, the two of them content, married a long time. Quiet but blazing hearth. And if I brought in a noise, dishevelment, the house disposed of it. We'd assembled to talk and eat.

I drove back to Oakland bathed unnameably. At home nothing had been altered, and yet, I tried to think, something had shifted. One or two degrees.

I sat with my eyes closed, took a pill. I went out walking.

I shaved, took a bath, opened all the windows. Someone called from the rose garden. Her words sound and rarely echo. I went driving again, bought a pack of cigarettes, removed one, set the pack on the sidewalk outside the liquor store, got back in the car, started it, lit the cigarette, rewound the OutKast, drove down an avenue peaceful, pained.

Through the small window one sees a dark window of the neighboring house. I write this surrounded now by each of these windows.

A trembling as something becomes thirsty, begins to dismantle, unbraids, wants to break. You dream that your free revealing isn't believed. You're coaxed and charmed, someone steals in, ransacks and disarrays, and in the end doesn't want what he has uncovered. I am walking again. You dreamt of embracing someone. I thrust my tongue inside, I taste what to another would be perhaps repellent, my tongue pulls out then plunges back in, a pair of eyes is open and two ears are flushed.

Easter. Sense is disabled. I am now several blocks from home. A letter's stupid words betray their incomprehension.

Two faces occupied by kissing.

Drone vehemently, regurgitate. Sound of a shovel striking soil.

Scent of cum and chewing gum. Head flung back. Narcissus by a doctor's window.

If you had truly entered, you would have found something, the letter says. But spring comes, and the magnolia blossom, cut and situated against a water-shot, dirty window, will maintain its shape and color only a little while longer.

And before I sleep I want to draw at last from that single day, which is then, today, and tomorrow. I lay on a plaid wool blanket in hot green grass, near a fence covered by pumpkin-colored blossoms. Between my face and those boughs that seemed to steam pollen, fly-like bugs circuited steadily. They went on and on like that. All I saw and felt made possible by the sun. And then night falls incrementally. Mirrors become available. A robin mates with a robin and makes another robin. Seed mates with earth and makes a flower. A rope mates with a beam and the sun is extinguished.

White Tower

We can burn it
It's infected
fields, records, our fruit
water, mosques, it casts inordinate shadow
I have a lighter, you have fuel
Hatefully designed, well-defended, it kills, sells
We won't try to climb, we douse
the perimeter, flood the subfloors with fuel
We drench the lobby
White tower that sodomizes horizons

Farewell Antithesis

Wild dogs in a pack, matted fur
mad eyes, maybe rabid

The sun's explosions hunt cold in the sand
and burn dirt paths the pack travels

Against a rock, black but seeming to flame
leans the weak white goat they're after

Gray long tongues and dirty foam on spiked vises
The guttural rumbling would be a swarm's sound

broadcast in a rainy canyon but for the sun
and the smallest dog's yelp

at the smell of feces, bowel oil licked
off the hot rock, meat tugged from bones

The noise of the pack or the smell of it
arouses the goat's alarm momentarily

then its head falls back against the rock
Attacked first in the ass and tail, whipped through the sand

One dog takes hold of its face, another crushes its throat
One sprays the rock a little in its fervor, another's tongue

bounces as it copulates a stray hole in the goat
whose eye confronts a malfunctioning sun

One dog attacks the back of another's head
One turns and assaults the rock, one unwittingly shits

on the dismantled rib cage
In the distance ripe dates are eaten by rats and ants

horizon and river share a comely cyan
One has a carrion bird by the wing and wags

Spirals

A thoroughly new structure, sunlit, immaculate
A savvy curation of objects, appropriate in number
Gray polished concrete walkways, a Tàpies
Tall walls of pigmented plaster
Brushed aluminum and slabs of light aqua
Library ladders, catalogs, tiled pool
Rooms like sites, one creamy, warm
in the crib serpents and worms

Snuff Philippians

I am confident of this, that the one who begins work
on you will continue until it is complete
"Does he hear my words?"
Go on, ask the embalmer
But with him you're silent
he won't hear your voice
you know why his notes belittle you
You gave your own health in order
that Brahmins and butchers should hang together
Missionary music with treated seasound, treated gunfire
If you'd scrubbed the honeysuckle from your neck
and poisoned a Brahmin's flock   the earth absorbs
transmissions from frontmatter to dead animal
Displayed like this, formatted to dissuade a boy growing
from effable death collecting

He must remove your heart, so will continue
but even cremated you'll invade bodies
resident at rich addresses

for that single eyelash stuck to the glass
of a Mexican pastry shop
And then you'll invade gardens of rich addresses
in order that the eyelash
may once again attach
to its face.

This table's steel is tenderer
than a hundred rich addresses
Let their own sons foam away
and be dropped from an immense safe
into that gulf
replenished now and forever by fluid removed

Limbs of Life

Gazing at flame in a locked room
unable to leave, sleepless, relieved only in daydream
I reanimate a bed in which I'd lain
loveless and ill once
and heard somewhere outside
provocative, despondent song
whose source I soon sought
and found high up in a nest
I struggled to reach   I thought
This creature is also not well
With each higher bough I mounted
the coal-colored bird also climbed
For weeks I brought it seed
bread crumbs, grubs, honey
fudge, crushed nuts, each morning
replenishing a fresh dish
and its caution turned slowly to trust
It was caught, carried home, put into a cage

in a small room from which care had been taken
to remove other such cages
A bird released will resume its flight
as in flameshapes I see gold trees again
and red

Fountain

Here she is, anything can be asked of her
Pinkish gravel underfoot
White behind a door before awaking, transferred
to a scene of empty lemon boughs
and for her face in this photograph
to be beauty before a day of inaugural travel
lying dying alongside a vast plain
a silver sky, cureless premonitions of
fluid thrust from the mouth
because she only wanted to escape the plain
move away from a sick lake
through lobbies of quiet ivory hotels
something hadn't expired inside
or floated past
The fountain sprays and sprays again the same water
Her lines, both horizontal and on glass
are assaulted by a coil's shadow
despite how well she has eaten now and sleeps
She'll want to rest by this fountain again

in an ironed cotton blouse gathered in at the sides
Never addressed, simply left alone to nap in warm grass
the clouds that advance toward her from the north
such a fresh white they don't frighten
and surely there will be nurses
who could come, like Chase's paintings of public spaces
winning, proportionate, sunblushed in the fashion
of autumn afternoons but for the desire
to travel back at night

Matthew 23:15

Jesus said: Woe unto you, scribes
and Pharisees, hypocrites!

for ye compass sea and land to make
one proselyte, and when he is made, ye make

him twofold more the child of hell
than yourselves

Blood Dub

for Christine Hume

Crave your arrival, crave summer lines
to sow inside, Inspirer
crave beads from the tiny vial
crescents and pink tongue
crave vibrations while dining
the salt slide, crave stunning oil
and salivation trails, wet curls
crave tasting the plum drug
a purple pearl on my ear
crave catlapping your lips
and the sun to swell as in the fable
of Jah's throb in a cherry aperture
and flood the folds

Entrance

The charms will change, elegy engines return as worms in this
grass, will cross from beneath zero to a living five

Three of it will be love. Born into sevens rich with raped sixes as
you will pass through the gate of all wonder without wanting

death will draw you to it though it will be life you lead
inside these rows. Block-long hedges. Hallways of leaves

alleys of boughs. Thickets
Naked in thickets, be killed in leaves

Heavy red sky then white sky, ice. You will become lost
I will be trying to eat flies. Openings will accept then want

to swallow
Though it will wound (magnets will pull out your heart)

soon the moon
only light in which to find you

orbic, wet, white, it will pour
You will absorb, it has always pulled

Spores, parasites, gunbutts, photographs. Orbic, spilling, irises
of sea-ice blue

An ally in a maze
that will stay exitless each lane

more alive than the last. Long, tolerant aisles
innumerable branches, mounds

Walls flora of blackened green then not
orange, ugly uncanny blue that will want to seep

Plates of ice, frozen sand
Hedges of vegetal mass or concrete, or mirror, chain-

link rows, endless intenser red wood. Easiest exits deadly
doorways she will think to use to escape dogs, blows

Blackways. Endurance ecstasy early
evenings in blighted lanes you will find food

Bloody the nose of a dog, fall against a clump of
shrub that will be aflame and burn your

hand. You become lost
Blistered hand. Awaken how much later on dirt

of streambanks, without burns, awaken again in a fresher lane
Autumnal, flies frozen maggots alive

Lanes louder
fouler

than others, identical in breadth
Bats the same speed and bees of same noise

Aloneness severer
In this row you will easily breathe

Your brother will come here to breathe
In these havens

names will be forgotten. On an expanse of frost
you will be bitten, want to die

In a rainshower reminders
Turning back into a warm passageway

a blade has sprung from the leaves and slit
your shoulder, blades quickly back into hedge

Find a child dozing
Pools, snakes, swelling moon, foil, strangled cats, thirst

You will fall beneath sod
Vault littered with cocks, lies, teeth of fanatics, confused faces

fools wore, dogs will be dragged through tents
You will be suffocated almost to death, then given

air. You find me sleeping, sleep too
Find what you least need

The dog hung by its leash, content to hang until
a watchband glints again

and confused
it thrashes, will want to leap at anyone

or find what I most need, having lost my way
You love me. You will have lost your brother

and so much sleep
In several gardens dogs come to clean you

Leash remnants. Comb these dogs, show them
Thundershowers wash seeds from our hair

Lusted poisoning of men in sunstorms
Minutes of vision, months sick with memory

Burned curtains
cried down lanes after fragments of nightjacket

Did you see a white peak in the sky
Motes proliferate. A snake strikes at glass

will turn, strikes at your boot. I stamp it
eat it, eat mirror, swallow my tongue

Revived on an overlook
stand again, persuaded to survey

distance, find it ocean, wooded aisles
lies, false collage your thirst

that need to eat, to
love, live lost